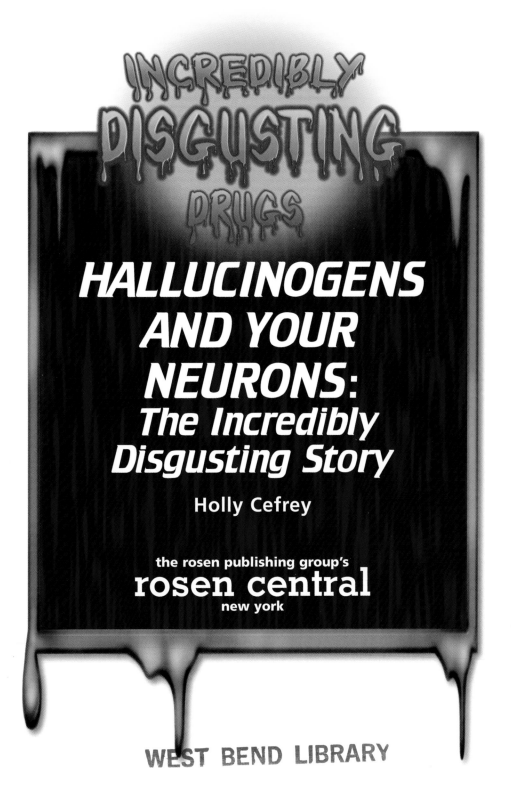

INCREDIBLY DISGUSTING DRUGS

HALLUCINOGENS AND YOUR NEURONS:
The Incredibly Disgusting Story

Holly Cefrey

the rosen publishing group's
rosen central
new york

Published in 2001 by The Rosen Publishing Group, Inc.
29 East 21st Street, New York, NY 10010

Copyright © 2001 by The Rosen Publishing Group, Inc.

First Edition

Library of Congress Cataloging-in-Publication Data

Cefrey, Holly.
Hallucinogens and your neurons : the incredibly disgusting story/ Holly Cefrey.—1st ed.
p. cm. — (Incredibly disgusting drugs)
Includes bibliographical references and index.
ISBN 0-8239-3391-1
1. Hallucinogenic drugs—Health aspects—Juvenile literature.
[1. Hallucinogenic drugs. 2. Drugs. 3. Drug abuse.] I. Title.
II. Series.
RM324.8 .C44 2001
615'.7883—dc21

                                                    2001000022

Manufactured in the United States of America

CONTENTS

Introduction

"My older brothers had been going to Memorial Park for years. One summer day, they decided to take me with them. That was the first time I tried pot. My brothers told me that they had been doing it for a long time, and offered it to me. We smoked and played Frisbee. It seemed like a cool way to spend an otherwise boring summer. I would wake up, go to the park, smoke, and veg out. Pretty soon I stopped going to the park. I'd just get up, smoke, and then hang out in the basement playing video games. My drug use, which at first had seemed like a new and exciting experience, became routine and started to bore me.

"I decided to return to the park, and try something new. I met a group of people that dropped acid. My oldest brother had tried it before and said that it was really wild. I asked a girl in the group if I could try some. She gave me a little strip of paper. She said, "You might try half a tab instead of a whole one, since it's your first time." I wanted to prove that I was cool so I took the whole tab. She told me to put it on my tongue and let it sit there. I did, and within a little while, my whole world changed.

"At first I had an uncontrollable urge to smile, so I did. I felt happy and everything that everyone was saying or doing seemed interesting. One of the girl's friends, named Pip, took a box of puppies from his van and brought it over. He was trying to find homes for the puppies, and he asked me if I wanted to name one of them.

"I suddenly started to feel a little overwhelmed. I looked toward the girl who had given me the acid, and I noticed that the patterns on her blouse seemed to be vibrating. Sounds became very sharp, and the sky seemed very bright. I didn't want to move, and suddenly I was too scared to look at anything other than my lap. I had heard about bad trips, and was a little worried that I might start having one. I told them that I wasn't sure what was going on, and they tried to calm me down. Pip put one of the puppies in my lap. 'Just pet him,' he said, 'and you will feel better.'

"I felt calm as the puppy squirmed in my lap. I petted it and was trying to think of a name for it. Before I knew it, Pip *snatched the puppy away from me and said, 'You're going to hurt it.' I thought that I was petting it gently, but I was really petting the puppy very hard—so hard that the puppy's eyelids were being stretched back, and it was whimpering.*

"It was a nightmare. I hurt an innocent thing, and everyone was looking at me like I was a freak. I couldn't get away fast enough, but I was so freaked out that I wasn't sure I could find my way home." —Ian, sixteen.

Ian's experience was caused by an illegal drug called a hallucinogen. As the name suggests, hallucinogens can cause a person to have hallucinations. A hallucination is when a person experiences something he or she believes to be real, even though it does not exist outside of that person's mind. Hallucinogens cause users to feel sensations, see things, and hear voices and sounds that do not exist.

Under the influence of hallucinogens, a person will experience a change in his or her understanding of self, direction, distance, time, or reality. A person cannot control the changes of understanding that occur during hallucinogenic drug use. Uncontrollable changes can cause disorientation. When a person is disoriented, it means that he or she has lost an understanding of the world around him or her. This can lead to frightening, harmful, and dangerous experiences for the user.

1 Hallucinogens: The Basics

Why do people use hallucinogens? It is a normal question to ask. After all, hallucinogens have been proven to be harmful. Unfortunately, our world is filled with substances that are bad for humans, but that are still used—and abused. There are several reasons why hallucinogens have been used in the past and are used today. The three main reasons for hallucinogenic use are spiritual, scientific, and recreational.

SPIRITUAL USE OF HALLUCINOGENS

Some historians believe that hallucinogens have been used for spiritual purposes since the time of the Aztecs. It is believed that Aztec spiritual leaders used hallucinogens for religious ceremonies. The leaders believed that the effects of the hallucinogens allowed them to communicate with their gods and with the spirit world.

Several tribes of Native North Americans have used peyote—a hallucinogen—in their religious ceremonies for hundreds of years. These tribes include the Huichol, Cora, and Tarahumara. Most of the tribes that use peyote during religious ceremonies are part of the Native American Church (NAC). The NAC practices the Peyote religion, which is over 10,000 years old.

The United States government allows the NAC to use peyote even though it is illegal. The NAC is allowed to use peyote because it is a part of their religion—the drug is not being abused. Members do not abuse the drug, as it is only used during religious rituals. Members of the NAC are urged by the church to avoid other drugs such as alcohol, and to live pure and healthy lives.

SCIENTIFIC USE OF HALLUCINOGENS

Scientists and psychiatrists have used hallucinogens in experiments to study and understand the human mind. During the 1950s and 1960s, medical professionals hoped

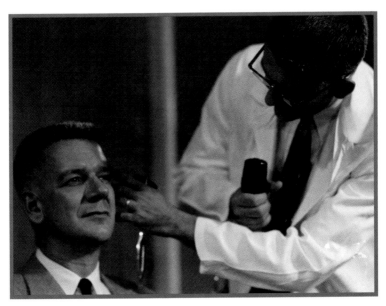

Scientists used hallucinogens in the 1950s and 1960s
in experiments to understand mental disorders.

that the use of hallucinogens in clinical tests would offer
a new understanding of mental disorders. Some hallucinogenic drugs, such as mescaline and LSD, were offered
by pharmaceutical companies to researchers specifically
for these studies.

After years of experiments, many doctors decided
that hallucinogens were not very helpful in understanding and treating mental illnesses. In 1965, Congress
passed the Drug Abuse Control Amendment, which
placed tight restrictions on hallucinogen research. Since
that time, the use of hallucinogens for medical research
has been very limited.

RECREATIONAL USE OF HALLUCINOGENS

Over the years, people outside of the scientific community have learned how to produce hallucinogenic drugs. These people have made the drugs available to the general public. Illegally sold drugs are known as street drugs. Using street drugs is a dangerous practice because these drugs can be improperly made and are sometimes mixed with other harmful substances. These substances can cause unexpected or deadly effects.

People who illegally use hallucinogenic drugs are called recreational users. Recreational users have a number of reasons for using hallucinogens. Many are attracted to the idea that the drugs can change the way they feel, or alter their behavior. These people believe that hallucinogen use offers new and interesting experiences. Some people suffering from depression have tried hallucinogens because they thought that it would make them feel less depressed. Many people say that they first used hallucinogens simply because they thought it would be fun.

The truth is that recreational use of hallucinogens is illegal and dangerous. For all of the reasons that people give to explain or justify recreational use, there are serious counterpoints to consider.

People offer many reasons as to why they use hallucinogens. But for each of these reasons, consider the counterpoints.

● I use because I want to experience new and interesting things.

    Did you know that even one wrong dose of a hallucinogen can cause severe brain damage? Damage to the brain, such as ruptured blood vessels, can affect many important bodily functions such as speech, vision, hearing, and memory. Even a one-time use of a hallucinogen can cause dramatic behavioral changes. These changes can last long after the drug has left the body; some are even permanent. Common side effects of recreational hallucinogenic use are memory loss and difficulty with speech. Why take something for a new experience if it can change you for the worse, forever?

● Using hallucinogens helps me to feel less depressed.

    Did you know that people who take hallucinogens often experience their natural emotions but on a stronger level? People who are depressed will often become severely depressed while using hallucinogens. Hallucinogen use has even led some people to commit suicide. In fact, depression is one of the more common side effects of recreational hallucinogen use. Why take something to cure depression that will only make you more depressed in the long run?

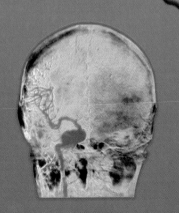

Just one wrong dose of a hallucinogen can cause blood vessels in the brain to rupture.

● I use hallucinogens because it is fun.
   Did you know that the effects of a hallucinogen can last well beyond twelve hours? The drug's duration and effect on your body cannot be predicted. While on hallucinogens, you can experience a wide array of uncontrollable emotions, some of which can cause you to do dangerous and harmful things. Why would you give control of your mind and body to something that is known to be harmful?

2 Types of Hallucinogens

There are over 100 substances that are used as hallucinogens. Hallucinogens can be found in nature or they can be made by humans. Hallucinogens found in nature are found in plants. Hallucinogens taken from plants are natural substances. Natural substances are called plant extracts.

Some hallucinogens come from plant extracts that have been chemically altered. These hallucinogens are partially synthetic, or semisynthetic. These substances have been chemically enhanced to produce hallucinogenic effects. Hallucinogens that are completely made by humans are called synthetic. Synthetic hallucinogens are chemically made in laboratories.

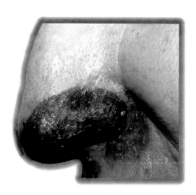

Snorting drugs can damage the cells in and around your nose.

There are also some substances from other drug categories, such as amphetamines, that have been known to cause hallucinations. Amphetamines are stimulants, which means that they make a person more active. Under certain circumstances, drugs like amphetamines can produce hallucinogenic effects.

Users take hallucinogens in a variety of ways. Hallucinogens are snorted through the nose, injected with a syringe, smoked, swallowed, chewed, or mixed with other substances. The way that a hallucinogen is taken most often, and the form that it's sold in, depends on the individual drug.

NATURAL HALLUCINOGENS

Mescaline

Mescaline comes from a cactus called peyote. It is a powerful drug that is known to cause users to become very sick. Most users take mescaline orally, and many soon regret doing so, as extreme nausea is a common side effect of mescaline use.

All hallucinogen use is dangerous, but users who inject hallucinogens directly into their veins run even greater health risks. Repeated injections have been known to cause Myositis Ossificans, the formation of calcified tissue (calcium deposits) in the muscles. Gross! Dirty needles also cause users to develop bone infections, and infected sores often develop at the site of injection.

Many users who inject have also been infected with serious diseases such as viral hepatitis. This disease is difficult to cure and causes serious liver damage.

Scarred injection sites can be seen on the forearm of an intravenous drug abuser.

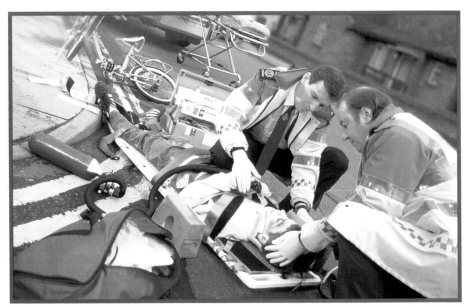

You could end up needing emergency medical care
if you mistakenly eat poisonous mushrooms.

Some users have been known to inject mescaline into
their skin with a syringe, or needle. This is especially
dangerous, as infections often occur at the site of injection.
In many cases, people who inject drugs face even more
disgusting problems. Serious infections are a common side
effect of injecting drugs.

Psilocybin/Psilocin (Magic Mushrooms, 'Shrooms)

Psilocybin and psilocin are the hallucinogenic drugs
found in some mushrooms. These drugs are powerful
and dangerous. Many users of these drugs have become

very physically and mentally ill. Nausea and extreme paranoia are common side effects of these two drugs.

Even more dangerous is the fact that users often mistake poisonous mushrooms for the mushrooms that contain psilocybin and psilocin. Different types of mushrooms look surprisingly alike. Many users have found themselves in the hospital emergency room after accidentally eating poisonous mushrooms.

SEMISYNTHETIC HALLUCINOGENS

LSD (Acid, Red Dragon, Green Dragon)

LSD stands for lysergic acid diethylamide. It comes from a natural acid called lysergic acid. Lysergic acid is found in a fungus called ergot. The ergot fungus commonly grows on rye grains.

Many people have been accidentally poisoned by eating rye grains with ergot fungus on them. Ergot poisoning is a painful ordeal. People become very sick and experience extreme mental confusion. Many people describe ergot poisoning as feeling like they are going to die.

Not surprisingly, since LSD comes from ergot, many people who have taken the drug experience effects similar to those of ergot poisoning. LSD users often suffer from terrible stomach cramps. They also feel extremely paranoid and have horrible hallucinations. Many people who have taken LSD feel like they are going insane and fear that they will never feel normal again.

Some drug users get their high by dissolving pieces of blotting paper soaked in LSD on their tongues.

SYNTHETIC HALLUCINOGENS

Hallucinogens that do not occur in nature are called synthetic hallucinogens. These drugs are made in illegal laboratories, often in very dirty conditions. Most illegal drug labs are filthy places. Oftentimes they are infested with rats and mice, and it is not unusual for mouse droppings to be found on the same tables on which the chemicals used in the drugs are mixed.

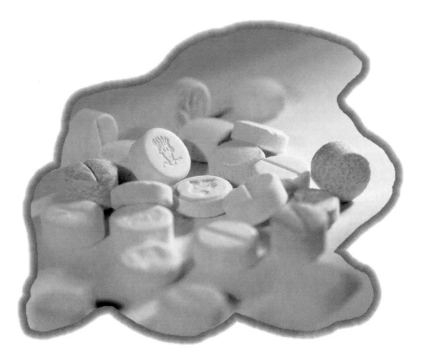

Some users break apart ecstasy tablets and snort them instead of swallowing them.

MDMA (Ecstasy, X, E, Adam)

MDMA is commonly referred to as ecstasy. MDMA is known as a mind-altering drug. Its chemical structure and effects are similar to hallucinogens and amphetamines. It is made in powder form and turned into tablets, and is most often white, yellow, or brown. MDMA is usually swallowed, but it is also injected. Some users break apart pills of MDMA and snort them.

PCP (Angel Dust, Loveboat)

PCP was used as a painkiller in the 1950s. PCP is not a true hallucinogen, but it's occasionally included in the hallucinogenic drug group. PCP is often mixed in with other drugs such as tobacco, cannabis, and cocaine. Many people take PCP without knowing it, since it can be mixed in with another drug they are taking.

PCP is an extremely dangerous drug. Some people who take PCP often become extremely violent. In some cases, people on PCP who have been picked up by the police due to their violent behavior seriously injure themselves trying to escape. People have been known to tear the skin off of their own hands trying to get free of police handcuffs.

3 Hallucinogens and You: The Disgusting Truth

As you have read, there are a lot of hallucinogens, and they are all illegal. Only researchers who have been given permission by the government and members of the Native American Church are allowed to use hallucinogens without being prosecuted. Besides the fact that hallucinogens are illegal, there is another really good reason not to do them—all hallucinogens are dangerous to your health.

Scientific tests have proven that hallucinogens can cause permanent damage to the brains of laboratory animals. Many scientists believe such brain damage occurs in human users of hallucinogens as well. A number of studies have even linked genetic damage to the

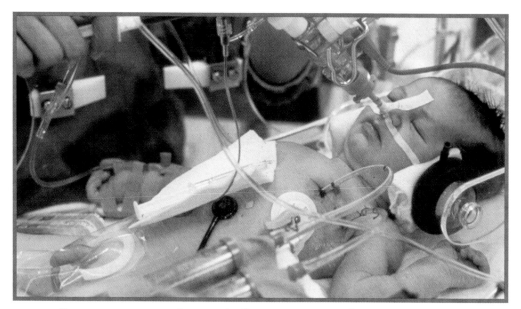

Pregnant women who use hallucinogens run the risk of giving birth to children with birth defects.

use of hallucinogens. This means that users of hallucinogens increase the chances that their children may be born with birth defects.

RESEARCHING HALLUCINOGENS

Researching the hallucinogenic drug group is a relatively new science. Exactly how hallucinogens do what they do is yet unknown. Studies have shown that certain cells and chemicals in the brain are affected while hallucinogens are being used. These cells and chemicals are an important part of a properly functioning brain. When the cells and chemicals are affected by hallucinogens, the brain cannot function properly.

The cells that are affected by hallucinogens are called neurons. Neurons are the cells of the nervous system. The nervous system is responsible for communicating messages between the body and the brain. These messages allow us to understand and react to our environment. Neurons use different chemicals to relay and react to messages. The chemical that is affected by hallucinogens is called serotonin.

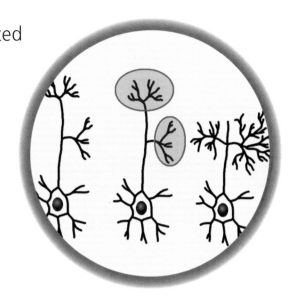

Hallucinogens damage the brain's neurons. The illustration shows a healthy neuron (left), where hallucinogens damage the neuron (shaded area on the middle image), and abnormal growth afer damage (right).

RESEARCHING SEROTONIN

Researchers have studied serotonin since the 1950s. Researchers have found that serotonin plays a part in our emotions and judgment. Studies have also linked our ability to sleep, our moods, and our appetite to serotonin. It has been proven that the amount of serotonin in the brain is directly related to our behavior.

Researchers have found that hallucinogens cause serotonin to be released from neurons in large amounts. As hallucinogenic use continues, the level of serotonin available in the brain is lowered, or depleted. Low levels of serotonin have been linked to various kinds of behavioral problems. Violent, aggressive, irrational, and suicidal behaviors have all been linked to low serotonin levels in the brain. This may account for the fact that hallucinogen users often experience depression as a side effect of the drug.

"I was released yesterday from the hospital. My parents don't want me to hang out with my best friend anymore. They think that it's his fault that I was taken to the emergency room. I know that it's really my fault. I didn't have to try PCP. I could have said no, but I didn't.

"I remember the party—I basically remember all of it. I had a lot of time in the hospital to think about what happened, and what I had done. Stu, my best friend, offered me some PCP. I had been drinking too. Maybe I would have been able to say no if I hadn't already been a little wasted. Instead, I took it.

"I was really out there. I was happy one minute, and really angry the next. I ran around Stu's pool throwing the patio furniture into it. I ran upstairs to Stu's bedroom and broke some of his things. I thought that someone was

24

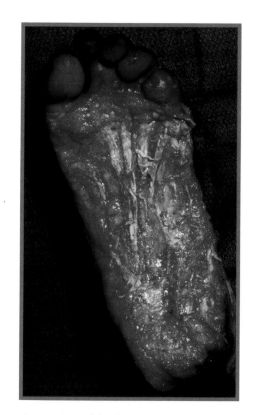

Irrational behavior brought on by the use of PCP can lead to serious injuries.

coming to get me and hid in his closet. My heart started pounding and I couldn't breathe. I started screaming for someone to help me. Stu came up and opened the closet door. I pushed past him and opened his window, climbing out onto the roof.

"Stu followed, trying to grab my leg. I kicked him away from me and ran to the edge of the roof. Down below, I could see the pool. It was glistening and calm. My heart ached and I couldn't take it anymore. I thought that the pool would save me. I jumped. I know that it sounds stupid, but at the time, it seemed to make sense. I landed on the pavement steps leading into the pool. I awoke a day later in the hospital, after surgery.

"My doctor told my parents that I was lucky. She said that the broken bones from the fall are the least harmful things that I did to myself that night. She said that PCP causes comas and heart failure, and that I was lucky to be conscious.

"She has ordered me back for tests, because they have to make sure that I haven't caused permanent damage to my brain. She says that I will also have to go to physical therapy for the next few months to make sure that I heal properly. I have a whole new set of problems to think about now because of a choice that I made in one stupid second." —Tricia, fifteen.

Tricia's experience shows what can happen when hallucinogens affect the brain. The brain is your command center. It is directly responsible for who you are and what you do. Hallucinogens disrupt your command center: They can alter your understanding of who you are and what you do. Different hallucinogens affect the brain in different ways. More research is needed in order to understand everything about the different kinds of hallucinogens, but there are some potential effects that all hallucinogens have in common:

- Disorientation; a sense of loss and isolation
- Feelings of anxiety
- Feelings of paranoia
- Feelings of depression
- Mental confusion
- Loss of thought control
- Violent behavior

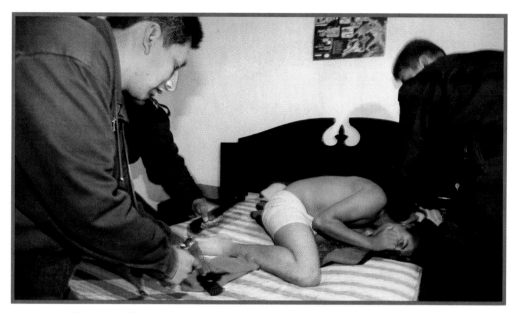
Police officers try to restrain a teen on drugs.

Hallucinogens are also known to cause flashbacks. Flashbacks are moments—long after the initial drug use—when a person reexperiences certain sensations that occurred during the drug use. When and how a flashback occurs is unpredictable. Flashback episodes can be frightening and stressful. They can occur even years after the initial drug experience, or trip.

Studies have shown that higher doses of hallucinogens are more likely to cause hallucinations and flashbacks than low doses. High doses of hallucinogens are also known to cause:

● Catatonic states: extremely still or extremely violent periods of behavior

- Permanent changes in mental ability
- Permanent changes in the nervous system and physical reactions
- Ruptured, or exploded, blood vessels in the brain
- Convulsions
- Coma
- Death

Because your brain controls the rest of your body, hallucinogens also affect the body when they are at work in the brain. Hallucinogens affect the parts of your brain responsible for your body's coordination. They also affect areas directly related to your heart and breathing. Just as there are known effects of hallucinogens on your brain, there are known effects of hallucinogens on your body:

- Increased blood pressure (overworked heart)
- Convulsions
- Heart failure (the heart stops working)
- Lung failure (the lungs stop working)
- Coma

4 The Unpredictable Dangers

One of the greatest dangers of hallucinogens is the fact that they have very unpredictable effects. The same type of hallucinogen can affect different people in very different ways. In fact, even the same person can have very different experiences each time he or she takes the same drug. Like any other drug, the effects of a hallucinogen depend upon many factors.

How Much of the Drug Is Taken

All drugs can produce dangerous side effects. When doctors prescribe medicine to their patients, they know exactly how large each dose should be. The correct amount varies from person to person. Doctors are trained to know how much medicine to give each patient.

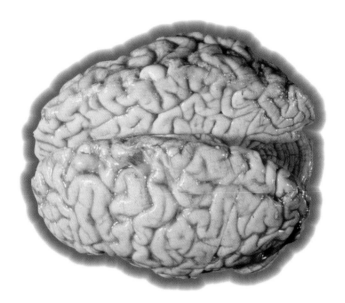

Hallucinogens can raise your heart rate and blood pressure high enough to rupture the blood vessels in your brain.

With hallucinogens, users blindly make the choice of the amount of drug they want to take. This is a huge problem, as it is difficult to judge the difference between a small dose and a large dose. Oftentimes, the user will take too much of the hallucinogen, producing serious and harmful results.

Due to the high blood pressure and increased heart rate caused by hallucinogenic drug use, even a healthy person can experience a stroke. Strokes cause permanent brain damage and often leave victims paralyzed. Blood pressure sometimes becomes so elevated during hallucinogen use that blood vessels in the brain rupture.

There are further complications to consider. Since hallucinogens are made illegally—and without regulation—two seemingly similar amounts of the same drug can contain more or less of a hallucinogen. There is no way to know how much LSD a piece of blotter paper contains, or how much MDMA a tablet of ecstasy has in it, until it is taken.

Hallucinogen use can cause severe damage to your liver.

The Way in Which the Hallucinogen Is Taken

Most hallucinogens can be taken in a few different ways. The way that a hallucinogen is taken can produce different side effects, even if it's the same drug. For example, when users sniff or snort hallucinogens, they often experience bleeding and infections in their nasal cavities.

If the Hallucinogen Is Mixed with Other Substances

Other substances can change the effects of a hallucinogen. Mixing any combination of drugs is very dangerous and risky, and this is especially true with hallucinogens. Hallucinogens taken by themselves are very unpredictable, so adding other drugs such as alcohol to the mix is a sure recipe for disaster.

Mixing drugs is also very dangerous to the liver. The liver is the organ in your body that filters out toxic substances. Since hallucinogens are highly toxic, a user's liver must work very hard to rid the body of the toxins. Livers become damaged when there are too many toxins in the body to filter out. Mixing hallucinogens with other drugs, such as alcohol, increases the damage to the liver.

The User's Hallucinogenic History

Repeated use of certain hallucinogens causes a user to build up a tolerance to the drug. This means that the user has to take more of the drug each time to produce the same effect. This causes the user further problems, as stronger doses usually lead to stronger side effects.

The User's Mental State

The user's mood at the time that he or she takes the drug can be a major factor in how the hallucinogen affects that person. If a person feels paranoid or scared, a hallucinogen will most likely heighten the feelings. Mild anxiety can become extreme paranoia under the influence of a hallucinogen.

5 The Effects of Hallucinogens

All types of hallucinogens have known side effects. Side effects are different for each drug. The effects that happen during a drug's use will vary from person to person. Some people will develop a couple of effects while others may develop all of the effects. There is no way of predicting which combination of side effects a hallucinogen will cause, but certain effects are linked to each drug.

Mescaline

Many samples of mescaline have been found to contain PCP and LSD. Mescaline can produce the following side effects:

- Nausea
- Vomiting

Nausea and vomiting are common side effects of mescaline.

- Low blood pressure
- Heart problems (slowing of the heart rate)

Psilocybin

Psilocybin is a hallucinogen found in certain types of mushrooms. Very often such drugs as LSD and PCP are misrepresented as psilocybin. Known effects of psilocybin are:

- Fatigue
- Feelings of isolation
- Dizziness and lightheadedness
- Stomach discomfort
- Numbness of tongue, lips, or mouth

- Nausea
- Anxiety
- Shivering
- Sweating

LSD

LSD has been known to cause users to do dangerous, irrational things, such as jumping out of windows or stepping in front of moving vehicles. LSD is also commonly known to produce flashbacks. An LSD flashback can occur days, weeks, and even years after LSD use. Other known effects of LSD include:

- Increased blood pressure
- Rapid heartbeat
- Stomach pain and severe cramping
- Muscular weakness
- Trembling
- Nausea, loss of appetite
- Chills
- Hyperventilation (difficulty with breathing)
- Panic
- Depression

- Anxiety
- Difficulties with sleep

MDMA

Research studies on animals injected with MDMA have shown that MDMA damages and destroys certain brain cells. Other known effects of MDMA are:

- Hallucinations
- Confusion
- Depression
- Problems with sleep
- Extreme anxiety
- Paranoia

DMT

The effects of DMT are similar to LSD (see LSD effects). DMT is also known to cause heightened levels of anxiety or panic in its users.

MDA

Users who take high doses of MDA will most likely need emergency medical care. High doses often lead to serious or deadly side effects. Deaths and near deaths have occurred due to MDA use. Other known effects of MDA are:

- Dilated pupils
- Dry mouth and nose
- Increased blood pressure
- Physical exhaustion with feelings of anxiety

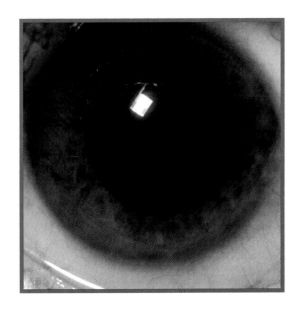

Dilated pupils are a common side effect of MDMA abuse.

PMA

High doses of PMA have caused users to go into comas or die. Other known side effects of PMA include:

- Increased heart rate (overworked heart)
- Increased blood pressure
- Increased and troubled breathing
- High body temperature
- Uncontrollable eye movements

- Muscle spasms
- Nausea and vomiting

STP

STP is known to produce severe reactions, or bad trips. STP is known to cause psychotic reactions among users who have existing mental disorders. Other side effects of STP are:

- Dry mouth
- Facial flushing
- Nausea
- Blurred vision
- Sweating
- Shaking
- Exhaustion
- Confusion
- Sleeplessness
- Delirium (mental disturbance)
- Convulsions

TMA

Researchers have yet to study the side effects of TMA. It is known that TMA causes mescaline-like hallucinations.

PCP

PCP is an extremely dangerous drug. PCP is known to cause delusions and severe mental turmoil in its users. Many people who use PCP become violent and pose a threat to themselves and others. People who use PCP for long periods of time experience memory loss and difficulties with speech. High doses of PCP have led to death or near-death experiences. Other known effects of PCP are:

- Increased heart rate
- Facial flushing
- Muscle stiffness
- Lack of coordination
- Drowsiness
- Confusion
- Numbness in the arms and legs
- Nausea and vomiting
- Sweating
- Feelings of isolation
- Violent behavior

6 Saying "No!" to Disgusting Drugs

If you come into contact with hallucinogens, remember what they can really do to your brain and body. Just because you know someone who has had a good trip doesn't mean that you will. These drugs are very unpredictable and can lead to injury and even death. Also, some hallucinogens are addictive, which means that you won't be able to say no as easily after the first use.

Many people are introduced to hallucinogens through family members or friends who use hallucinogens. If your family member or friend doesn't accept the answer no, remind him or her of the following facts.

Hallucinogens are illegal. If caught with hallucinogens, you will most likely face costly fines or time in jail.

Hallucinogens are dangerous. Doing hallucinogens increases the chances of injuries. Falls, burns, drownings, and suicides have all been linked to hallucinogen use. Hallucinogens have also been shown to cause permanent brain damage in users.

One use can change you for life. A wrong amount of any hallucinogen can cause permanent mental or physical problems.

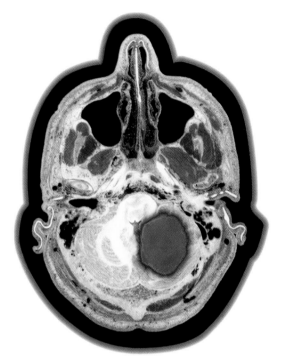

Hallucinogen abuse may cause internal bleeding in the brain, which can lead to a stroke—the death of brain tissue.

Hallucinogens are more trouble than they are worth. Drugs can put your health, intelligence, family, and friends at risk for potential damage or ruin.

Hallucinogens won't make life better. Hallucinogens won't make you more grown-up, more popular, or more likeable. In fact, hallucinogens may hinder your chances of success in life.

GLOSSARY

anesthetic   A painkilling or sensation-numbing medicine.

amphetamine   The name for a group of drugs that have a stimulant effect.

crystalline   Made of, or looking like clear rocks. Substances can be naturally crystalline or chemically changed into a crystalline state.

disorientation   A feeling of being lost.

flashback   When a person reexperiences certain sensations that occurred during hallucinogenic drug use.

hallucination   An experience of something that does not exist outside of the mind; an illusion.

hallucinogen   A substance that causes a hallucination.

nerve   Bundles of fibers that form a system connecting the brain and spinal cord with other parts of the body and relay information throughout the system.

neuron   A nerve cell, part of the nervous system.

perception   A person's understanding of something.

plant extracts   Substances taken from plants.

reality   Something real, or the state of being real.

senses Parts of the human body that allow a person to understand and interpret his or her surroundings. The five main senses are vision, touch, taste, hearing, and smell.

serotonin The chemical of the nervous system linked to emotion, judgment, moods, and sleep.

synthetic Manufactured; made by humans.

tolerance A gradual buildup of resistance to the effects of a drug.

trip A term used to describe the experience of taking a drug.

FOR MORE INFORMATION

In the United States

American Council for Drug
   Education
164 West 74th Street
New York, NY 10023
(212) 758-8060
(800) DRUG HELP (378-4435)
Web site:
   http://www.acde.org

Center for Substance Abuse
   Treatment
5600 Fishers Lane
Rockville, MD 20857
Information and treatment
   referral hotline:
   (800) 622-HELP (4357)
Web site: http://www.samhsa.
   gov/centers/csat/csat.html

National Clearinghouse for
   Alcohol and Drug
   Information
P.O. Box 2345
Rockville, MD 20847-2345
(301) 468-2600
(800) 729-6686
Web site:
   http://www.health.org

NAFARE Alcohol, Drug, and
   Pregnancy Hotline
200 N. Michigan Avenue
Chicago, IL 60601
(800) 638-BABY (2229)

Narcotics Anonymous (NA)
World Service Office
P.O. Box 9999
Van Nuys, CA 91409

(818) 773-9999
Web site: http://www.na.org

National Council on
    Alcoholism and Drug
    Dependence
20 Exchange Place,
    Suite 2902
New York, NY 10005
(800) NCA-CALL (622-2255)
Web site:
    http://www.ncadd.org

National Families in
    Action (NFIA)
Century Plaza II
2957 Clairmont Road, Suite 150
Atlanta, GA 30329
(404) 248-9676
Web site: http://www.national
    families.org

In Canada

Addiction Research Foundation
33 Russell Street
Toronto, ON M5S 2SI
(800) INFO-ARF (463-6273)
(416) 595-6111
Web site: http://www.arf.org

Canadian Centre on
    Substance Abuse
75 Albert Street, Suite 300
Ottawa, ON K1P 5E7
(613) 235-4048
Web site: http://www.ccsa.ca

Web Sites

National Institute on
    Drug Abuse
http://www.nida.nih.gov

National Institute on Drug
    Abuse: Hallucinogens
http://www.nida.nih.gov/MOM/
    HALL/MOMHall1.html

National Substance Abuse
    Web Index (NSAWI)
http://nsawi.health.org/compass

FOR FURTHER READING

Algeo, Philippa. *Acid and Hallucinogens*. Danbury, CT: Franklin Watts, 1990.

Hurwitz, Sue, and Ann Ricki Hurwitz. *Hallucinogens*. Rev. ed. New York: The Rosen Publishing Group, Inc.,1999.

Kuhn, Cynthia, Scott Swartzwelder, and Wilkie Wilson. *Buzzed: The Straight Facts About the Most Used and Abused Drugs From Alcohol to Ecstasy*. New York: W.W. Norton and Company, 1998.

Robbins, Paul R. *Hallucinogens*. Springfield, NJ: Enslow Publishers, 1996.

Sevastiades, Patra McSharry. *Danger: Hallucinogens*. New York: PowerKids Press, 1997.

INDEX

CREDITS

About the Author

Holly Cefrey is a freelance writer, researcher, and artist. She has written a variety of books for children and teens, covering such topics as medicine, science, history, and self-help.

Photo Credits

Cover, pp. 12, 15, 18, 19, 41 © Photo Researchers, Inc.; p. 9 © Bettmann/Corbis; pp. 14, 22, 25, 30, 31, 37 © CMSP; p. 16 © VCG/FPG; p. 27 © Associated Press; p. 34 © Cindy Reiman.

Series Design

Laura Murawski